Spin Class

It was a typical Tuesday morning for Jade. Out of bed at 5 a.m. then straight to the bike for a one-hour online spin class. She had always loved biking ever since she could remember. With her busy work schedule as lead engineer at a software development company, early morning spinning was her only time to break a sweat and clear her head.

"*This one kicked my butt,*" she thought as she did her last five minutes of cool-down, the drops of perspiration trickling down from her red hair onto the side of her face. She hit the shower, got dressed, and had a breakfast of steel-cut oatmeal with raspberries.

"*Better take the rain gear today.*" Jade rode her bike to work every day the five miles from her apartment into the city. It was sunny that morning, but rain was in the forecast later in the day. She wheeled her bike from her apartment, down the elevator, and out the apartment building door down the stairs to the street.

"See you later, Jade," the doorman said as he held the door open for her.

"Have a good day, Stan." As Jade started her ride she went through her calendar in her head. *"Stand-up team meeting at nine, customer meeting at 10, lunch with Kelly."* Kelly was the new vice president overseeing Jade's division. Jade was considered a rising star in the company, having been promoted five times in the 10 years since getting her BS in software engineering. Kelly made it a priority to meet with the high-potential employees in her organization. Jade was expecting a typical meet and greet with her new boss. Kelly had something more in mind.

BEHIND GOLD DOORS

SEVEN STEPS
TO CREATE A
DISABILITY
INCLUSIVE
ORGANIZATION

Lonnie Pacelli

Published by Pacelli Publishing
Bellevue, Washington

Pacelli
PUBLISHING

BEHIND GOLD DOORS
SEVEN STEPS TO CREATE A
DISABILITY INCLUSIVE ORGANIZATION

Published by Pacelli Publishing
9905 Lake Washington Blvd. NE, #D-103
Bellevue, Washington 98004
PacelliPublishing.com

ISBN-10: 1-933750-82-0
ISBN-13: 978-1-933750-82-8

Thai

Jade finished her customer meeting at 11:45. She had been thinking all morning about her lunch meeting with Kelly. Jade was typically comfortable around people, but Kelly was different. Like Jade, Kelly was a rising star in the company, the first woman to hold the position of vice president of software engineering. Jade knew the importance of first impressions, and while Kelly had a reputation as a very fair leader, Jade didn't want to blow it in her first meeting.

Jade headed over to Kelly's office. Kelly was just finishing up a call and motioned to her to come in and sit, then held up a one-minute finger while wrapping up her call.

"Yep . . . Good . . . Let's meet up on it tomorrow. Bye."

Kelly hung up the phone. "So nice to meet you Jade. You hungry?"

"Sure."

"Good. Let's skip the cafeteria. How about Thai?"

"Anything but the cafeteria."

Kelly smiled. "Agreed, let's go."

Kelly stood up, a tall, athletic-looking, put-together thirtysomething. She stood nearly a head taller than Jade; her imposing height adding to Jade's anxiousness.

The two small-talked during the three-block walk to the bustling Thai restaurant. The host greeted them as they walked in.

"Hello Kelly, your table's ready," he said.

"Thank you, Paul." Kelly and Jade followed Paul to the table.

"Your server will be by in a few to take your order."

"Great."

Kelly and Jade settled in and opened their menus.

"Do you have a favorite?" Kelly asked.

"Chicken Pad Thai."

"Done," Kelly said, closing her menu as the server approached.

"Chicken Pad Thai, zero spice please," Kelly said.

"Same but make mine two-spice."

Kelly smiled. "So you like some kick to it, huh?"

"Yeah, my father taught me how to eat spicy."

"Not me," Kelly said. "Spicy and I don't do well together, spicy always wins."

Kelly leaned forward, her palms on the table.

"Jade, I actually have a problem that I'd like you to think about helping me solve."

"Certainly, what can I do?"

"Last week I got the results of our employee survey, and I saw something that disturbs me. While folks are generally happy about their jobs, they feel that we are not inclusive of those with disabilities. The idea that anyone might not feel welcomed in our organization is something that bothers me greatly. I saw this firsthand growing up. My father was diagnosed with ALS when he was 30. First it was difficulty buttoning his shirt, then keeping his balance, then not being able to walk, then not being able to move at all. Even though his body was failing, his mind was as sharp as ever. There was so much more he had in him to contribute, but he just wasn't given the opportunity. It took watching my father die a broken man to make me a champion for people with disabilities."

Kelly took a deep breath and a sip of water to give herself a few seconds to compose herself. Jade sat leaning forward, elbows on table, clinging to every word.

Kelly continued. "I want our organization to be the disability inclusion gold standard that others inside and outside our company look to for how to create a disability inclusive organization. I want to create an initiative to change our disability inclusion DNA and I would like for you to lead it."

Whoa.

Jade didn't see that coming. Her expertise was in creating systems solutions that made people's lives better; it wasn't about changing an organization's culture. And besides, she never gave disability inclusion much thought. She wasn't against it, but she had never been passionate enough to advocate for it. Knowing Kelly's story and the expectations that went with it made her feel totally inadequate to take this on.

"Me? I'm an engineer; I've never done anything like this."

"Yes. Everyone I talk to about you speaks very highly about your ability to lead engineering teams. It's my job to ensure you are getting the right experiences to continue your growth as a leader. Leading a disability inclusion initiative would help meet that goal."

Jade rubbed along the back of her neck, feeling a bit of sweat at the nape. She did her best to not show her nervousness.

Kelly tried to set her at ease. "I know this sounds like a monumental task, and one that probably scares you."

"*That's an understatement,*" Jade thought to herself.

Kelly continued. "Rest assured I've got your back on this. Any problems, you let me know and I'll help you. How about you sleep on it and we'll talk more about it tomorrow?"

Jade was relieved she didn't have to give an answer on the spot. "That would be great."

"Good, tomorrow we'll get into details and give you more to think through before you decide." Just then the server came to the table holding two plates.

"Chicken Pad Thai no spice?" he said.

"That's mine." The server put the plate in front of Kelly, then the other in front of Jade.

"Enjoy," the waiter said as he left the table.

"Thank you," Kelly said. Kelly and Jade continued on with small talk through lunch and on the walk back to the office. Jade did the best she could to stay engaged, but Kelly's ask stuck in the back of Jade's mind. When they got back to Kelly's office; her next meeting was already waiting for her.

"Thanks for lunch, Kelly."

"Sure thing. We'll talk tomorrow."

"OK."

Rain Gear

For the rest of the day Jade couldn't get Kelly's story out of her mind. She had never known anyone close to her with a disability and couldn't imagine the pain Kelly felt watching her father die the way he did.

"*How could I possibly do this justice?*" she thought to herself. "*I'm an engineer, I build stuff. I don't have the experience to do this. What if I fail? I don't want to disappoint Kelly, knowing how important this is to her.*" Jade got up to get some water. On the way she looked outside at the dark clouds forming. "*Gonna need the rain gear tonight,*" she thought.

At 5:30 p.m. she packed up her stuff, slipped on her rain pants and jacket, and headed out. She walked by Kelly's office just as Kelly looked up and gave Jade a quick wave goodbye.

It was unusually dark for this time of year. The rain quickly went from a light mist to a torrential downpour. Jade had ridden in rain before, but nothing quite like this. "*Just go slow,*" she thought as she went through each intersection. She considered stopping and waiting it out, but there was no guarantee that it would let up. "*Halfway home. I can do this.*"

Then it happened.

Gold Doors

The walls, ceiling and floor were a gleaming white marble. Jade stood at one end of the hallway, still wearing her bike helmet and rain gear. She patted up her body--legs, then torso, then head. Just seconds ago she was soaked to the skin from the downpour.

"I'm dry. Where am I?"

Jade looked down the hallway. Three luminous gold doors lined each of the left and right walls with a seventh door at the far end of the light-filled corridor. She turned around to see only a marble wall behind her.

"How did I get in here?"

The seven gold doors each had three panels with a gold ring knocker at the door's center. The only distinguishing factor was the embossed number on each door--doors 1, 3, and 5 on the left and 2, 4, and 6 on the right. Door number 7 was at the end of the hallway.

"Seven doors? Why seven? Do I have to choose one?"

The room was still; so still that the only sound Jade could hear was the sound of her breathing.

"Is this heaven?"

She slowly started walking down the hallway; no sound of footsteps, only the sound of her inhales and exhales as she took each step. As she approached the first doors, door number 1 opened.

"Come in, Jade."

Binoculars

Jade cautiously approached the open door and looked inside. The room was quiet and dimly lit, with beige walls and ceiling, and light brown carpet. A fortyish woman with short brown hair sat behind a desk, typing on a notebook computer. "Sit, please," the woman said, still looking into her computer screen. Jade sat across from the woman, noticing how neat her desktop was; a far cry from Jade's messy desktop at work.

"Where am I?" Jade asked the woman.

"You're in my office."

"No, where AM I?"

"You're in my office."

Jade saw the futility of asking a third time. "OK, then who are you?"

The woman took her hands off the keyboard, clasped them, and set them in front of her on the desk. "My name is Anne," the woman said, still looking at her computer screen.

"Can you tell me what I'm doing here, Anne?"

"Why are you wearing a bike helmet?" Anne asked.

"I was riding my bike home then the next thing I know I'm in this weird place. Now can you tell me why I'm here? Am I dead?" Jade unbuckled the helmet and set it down by her chair.

"I'm not dead, so if you are then I'm talking to a ghost."

"*She won't even look me in the eye,*" Jade thought.

"Do you want to know why?" Anne said.

"Why what?"

"Why I won't look you in the eye."

"How did she know what I was thinking?" Jade asked herself.

"We can hear your thoughts here, so you might as well just say what you're thinking." Anne said.

"This is crazy!"

"You'll get used to it."

"Get USED to it? I'm here forever? What IS this place?"

Anne leaned back in her chair. "I'm the first of seven people you will meet to help prepare you for what is to come. We all know what Kelly asked of you and we want to give you the tools to help you succeed."

"You know about Kelly asking me to lead the disability inclusion initiative?"

"Yes. Now about your question of why I don't look at you. Looking into people's eyes is unpleasant for me; not because I'm not interested in you; it's just a lot of stimulation for me. It's kind of like if someone held a megaphone to your ear and started yelling; you wouldn't find that pleasant. That's how things are for me with not only looking in people's eyes, but also with unexpected sounds and even itchy clothing. My visual, hearing and touch sensors feel like they are magnified. Something that may not bother you at all could be excruciating for me. It's something that comes along with my disability."

"Your disability?" Jade asked.

"When I was four years old, I was diagnosed with autism spectrum disorder. At the time it was called pervasive developmental disorder-not otherwise specified but the American Psychiatric Association did away with that definition in 2012 along with another form of autism called Asperger syndrome. It's now called autism spectrum disorder, or ASD."

"I've heard of Asperger syndrome. It's not used anymore?" Jade asked.

"Clinically no, but a lot of people still refer to it. Got to keep to schedule, so I'll continue. My mother noticed when I was two that I wasn't saying very many words, so she sent me to a speech therapist. My mother also noticed some things in me that were different from my older sister. I could play for hours on end by myself. My favorite thing was to do puzzles. I would sit on the floor and do the same puzzle over and over again. It never got boring for me. Then there was the disruption in routine. I hate having my routine disrupted, even if it's what neurotypical people consider as fun. My pediatrician suggested to my mother that we see a doctor who specialized in developmental disabilities. The specialist confirmed I had autism spectrum disorder."

"Neurotypical?" Jade asked.

"It's a term used for people who aren't diagnosed with a developmental disorder, like autism. Just because I have autism doesn't mean how I think is better or worse. It just means I think differently. I'll give you an example. When I was younger my family and I were playing a game where you had to guess a word based on a description given. The word I got was 'binoculars.' I had to give my dad a description of the word without using the term 'binoculars' in it. I told him, 'two telescopes taped together.' He immediately got it. Everyone else was amazed at my description and how unique it sounded; to me it was perfectly logical. That is a good example of my being *neurodiverse*; I may think differently than others but it's not necessarily better or worse; just different. Now, we have a lot to cover and I only have eight more minutes until your next appointment."

"OK." Jade liked Anne's punctuality.

Anne continued. "Growing up was very difficult for me. At around seventh grade I started noticing that other kids had friends and did things together, yet no one asked me to do anything. I was never invited over to anyone's house to play, or to birthday parties. My mother and father tried hard to create situations where I could build friendships, but it was just too hard for me and other kids didn't want to put forth the effort. I spent a lot of my time pursuing whatever my latest obsession was--puzzles, a TV show, a toy, or a computer game. If I was interested in something, I could talk about it for hours, to a point where my parents would help me by saying, 'You can talk about this for another five minutes then we talk about something else.' That usually worked well for me. When I was in high school, I developed a passion for mathematics. Numbers made so much sense to me."

Anne hesitated for a moment then continued. "High school was so painful. I really wanted friends. I saw other kids going out for pizza, going to dances, and hanging out at the mall. There was only one person who considered me a friend, and she moved away during tenth grade. I just wanted to be considered part of the crowd. Instead, when I wasn't being completely ignored, I was being ridiculed by the other kids. I just wanted to fit in. I hated it."

"I'm so sorry things were tough for you," Jade said.

"They were extremely tough. Yes, I saw counselors and they helped me some, but the memories are still so painful. That's something else about me; my memories are extremely vivid and strong. Things that happened to me years ago feel like they happened just yesterday."

Anne reached over to grab a tissue from her desk. "Sorry, Jade, I didn't mean to get upset."

"It's totally fine, I feel so bad for you."

Anne wiped her nose with the tissue, threw it in the trash, and took a deep breath to collect herself.

"OK, enough of that. Back to math. I aced all my math classes and received a data science college scholarship. I earned a Ph.D. and now work as a data scientist for a social media company. It's great for me because I work independently doing what I love, crunching numbers. I've been offered managerial positions but know that the people aspects of that type of job would be too stressful for me, so I choose to work as an individual contributor."

"I wonder if Phil is on the autism spectrum?" Jade thought about Phil, one of her employees who always kept to himself, craved routine, and seemed uncomfortable in social situations.

"Yes, Phil is on the spectrum," Anne said.

Anne's response jarred Jade, having forgotten her thoughts were an open book in this strange place.

"In fact, there are some very successful people on the spectrum, including author Temple Grandin and actress Daryl Hannah. There's also speculation that Albert Einstein and Sir Isaac Newton were on the spectrum, but because the term autism wasn't first used until around 1911 and widespread diagnosis didn't occur until well after they died, they were never clinically diagnosed. Today about one in 54 children are somewhere on the spectrum, with 44 percent of them having average or above average IQs, like me. Boys for some reason are four times more likely than girls to be on the spectrum. In rare cases autism can be a result of things like herpes encephalitis, traumatic brain injury, or due to a baby's brain being deprived of oxygen before or during birth. Most times, though, the cause is unknown, and there is no known cure."

Anne looked at the clock on her desk. "Five minutes left."

"I have so many questions," Jade thought.

"Don't worry, all your questions will be answered."

"Right, the mind-reading thing again," Jade said.

"Now, on to the reason you're here. The seven of us are going to talk with you about seven important steps you will need to follow to create what we like to call a disability inclusive organization. I have a clipboard and pen for you to keep with you as you talk to us." Anne handed Jade the clipboard that held a sheet of paper with the words "Disability Inclusion" written across the top and the numbers one through seven down the side:

DISABILITY INCLUSION

1

2

3

4

5

6

7

Anne continued. "My job is to talk about the first step to create a disability inclusive organization. Before you can start on the journey of disability inclusion, it's important you have a clear understanding of what constitutes a disability. You'll also need to know some key statistics about disabilities, the stigmas, terminology, and attitudes about disabilities, and what's been done thus far to help those with disabilities thrive to the best of their abilities. The first step is *know the facts about disabilities*."

Jade looked at the single sheet of paper on the clipboard. "Do you have more paper? I won't be able to remember everything."

"I forgot, not everyone can remember facts like I can," Anne said. "For whatever reason, my ability to retain facts and data is like a computer database. I have a photographic memory and have no problem at all storing and retrieving huge amounts of data at a moment's notice. It's one of the things that makes me so good at my job. Even with my ability to recall facts and data, I have trouble with things like recognizing a person when seeing his or her face or with short-term memory. Something to know about people on the autism spectrum is that you can't generalize that we are all the same. While I am exceptionally good at remembering facts and data, someone else on the autism spectrum might have great difficulty with it."

Just as Jade was going to ask for the paper again, Anne continued.

"Now about writing down all the facts and stats; just write *DIchampion.com* in the upper right corner. What we tell you today will be available there to help you out later."

"DIchampion.com. Got it."

"Good. Now, onto the facts. According to the Center for Disease Control, a disability is any condition of mind or body that makes it more difficult for the person with the condition to do certain activities and interact with the world around them. A disability can present at birth, like Down syndrome. It can also be developmental, like autism. It could be related to an injury or associated with a longstanding condition like diabetes, which can lead to things like blindness. It could be progressive, like Parkinson's disease, static, like a limb loss, or intermittent like some forms of multiple sclerosis. One in four adults in the United States have some type of disability."[i]

"One in four?"

"Actually, it's 26 percent, sorry for not being more precise," Anne said.

Jade smiled. "26 percent is still a big number, much bigger than I would have thought."

"Yes, it is. However, with the facts come the stereotyping and stigmas. Those of us with disabilities could be viewed as having a poor quality of life, not being as healthy, or that something happened because of a personal tragedy or, even worse, as being punished for something done by us or a loved one. People with disabilities experience higher degrees of unemployment, with only 35 percent of adults with disabilities being employed. Children with disabilities are 3.7 times more likely to experience some type of violence than non-disabled children. They are also 3.6 times more likely to be victims of physical violence and 2.9 times more likely to be victims of sexual violence."[ii]

"My gosh." These last statistics hit Jade like a punch in the gut. The thought of any child being abused was bad enough, but to hear that it was so much more likely for a child with a disability made her want to retch.

Anne continued. "Through the years there have been significant pieces of legislation enacted to protect the rights of those with disabilities, including Section 504 of the Rehabilitation act of 1973, the Education for All Handicapped Children Act of 1975, the Americans with Disabilities Act of 1990, and the Patient Protection and Affordable Care Act of 2010. These pieces of legislation made strides in removing and reducing physical, medical, educational, and social barriers for people with disabilities, but even with this legislation there's still a long way to go until we can say we're truly inclusive of all abilities. Only one minute left, I have to keep to schedule. It's time to write down the first step on your clipboard."

Jade wrote down the first step to creating a disability inclusive organization:

```
┌─────────────────────────────────────────────┐
│                                               │
│  DISABILITY INCLUSION  * DICHAMPION.COM       │
│                                               │
│  1   KNOW THE FACTS ABOUT DISABILITIES        │
│                                               │
│  2                                            │
│                                               │
│  3                                            │
│                                               │
│  4                                            │
│                                               │
│  5                                            │
│                                               │
│  6                                            │
│                                               │
│  7                                            │
│                                               │
└─────────────────────────────────────────────┘
```

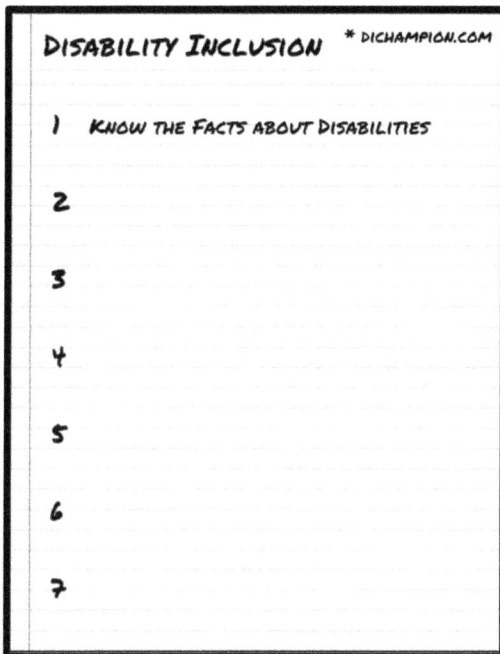

"Time for you to go, Jade."

Jade got up from her chair. "Thank you, Anne," Anne had already begun typing on her keyboard as Jade turned to leave.

"Good luck," Anne said, still staring at her computer screen, on to her next task.

Jade walked out of the room to hear a "Heya Jade!" coming from behind door number 2.

Strange Carving

Jade opened the door and squinted at the bright sun coming from the room. As she walked in she saw a simple log cabin with a burly man sitting in a rocking chair on its front porch. Another rocking chair sat next to him; a table with neatly arranged wooden carvings in between the chairs. The man was dressed in well-worn blue jeans and a flannel shirt. His leathery complexion was framed by a full head of black hair with graying temples and a bushy salt and pepper beard. He held a carving knife in one hand and a fresh piece of wood in the other.

"I've been looking forward to meetin' ya!" the man said. "Take a load off."

Jade made her way to the second rocking chair and sat. She slowly looked around at the log cabin, the porch, and then up at the sky. *I'm inside a room that's outside!* she thought.

"Yepper."

"Right, I forgot my thoughts are on display here. What's your name?"

"Gone by the name Buck for years. Birth name is Alfred, but never liked it. Only time I ever use Alfred is when I have to sign somethin' legal. Nothin' legal here, so call me Buck."

"Sure, good to meet you Buck."

"Good meetin' ya as well, Jade. How ya handlin' things so far?"

"Well it's been an experience."

"Just relax. Can I get ya somethin'?"

"I'm good, thank you," Jade said.

"Welp, let's get crackin' here." Buck put down the carving knife and wood piece on the table.

"So, I suspect Anne already talked with you about knowin' the facts about DI, huh?"

"She did."

"Bet she kept you to a pretty tight schedule huh?"

"Yes, down to the second."

Buck smiled with an affirming nod. "Yup, that Anne, she's amazin' for sure. Well I'm a bit more laid back here so just relax and let's just enjoy our chat. Bet you're wonderin' what we're gonna talk about."

"I'm wondering a lot of things right now."

"Well, first a bit more about me. I'm a third-generation logger. Grew up here in Washington state. Built this house with my own two hands. Been around white oak, red alder, and firs my whole life. Could swing an axe with the best of 'em. At about 43 years old, I noticed a tingling and pain in my feet and legs. Never gave it much thought; was part of the job. Let it go on for about a year and half and it wasn't goin' away. Jane, my better half, finally got me to a doc. He ran a bunch of tests, couldn't find anythin.' Then I had an MRI where they found lesions on my brain and spine. It was then he told me I had multiple sclerosis. That was, oh, about 15 years ago. Thought I'd be cuttin' down trees until the good Lord took me home like my daddy and granddaddy, but He had a different plan for me. Oh, I keep myself plenty busy; I let the young guys cut the trees down now. I've taken up carvin'. Got my own shop. I'll never be a millionaire but it keeps me busy and pays the bills."

"So, MS is considered a disability?" Jade asked.

"Well, suppose so if you're lookin' at clinical definitions. For me, it's just a turn in the road that I wasn't plannin' to take. But now that I'm on the road I'll just follow it."

"Do you have a lot of pain?"

"Some days it's just like I was out with my chain saw enjoyin' the beauty of nature. Then other days it's a lot of work just to get out of bed in the mornin'. Today is one of those days; can't stand for more than 10 minutes then gotta sit for a bit. I've gotten to be real good friends with this here rockin' chair."

"Do you take anything for the pain?"

"I just do an injection of this stuff called Rebif about three times a week. Jane used to have to do them for me but now I just do 'em myself. Even though I had to change a bit what I do, I still wake up each day countin' my blessin's."

29

"I have to say, Buck, you just seem to take things in stride. I admire your positive outlook."

"What do I have to be negative about? Gettin' thrown a curve when I was expectin' a fastball? Nah, it's all good. Me and Jane, we're doin' just fine."

Buck closed his eyes and rocked a couple of times while he gathered his thoughts. "Now let me tell ya about the second step in creatin' a disability inclusive organization. See, in the first step ya have to get a good understandin' about what disabilities are. But that's not enough to get people thinkin' about how to create a place where folks feel welcome and can thrive. Ya gotta make it clear why they need to do it. Ya need to *explain the why of DI.*"

"So, you mean you have to be able to clearly define the benefits of why an organization should be inclusive of all disabilities?"

"Yup. I'll give ya an example. There's a special unit in the Israeli Defense Force that watches for very small changes in troop movements using pictures from the sky. Every one of those soldiers is on the autism spectrum. The IDF found that soldiers on the spectrum are able to focus for longer periods of time without gettin' tired. They're able to do a job better and use their disability as an advantage."

"Really!" Jade said.

"Yessir. A couple years back a company called Accenture, you may be familiar with them?"

"Yes I am, good company." Jade said.

"See, Accenture did a study called 'Getting to Equal: The Disability Inclusion Advantage.' In this study they found some interestin' facts. That numbers lover, Anne, drilled me on these facts over and over again until I was sayin' 'em in my sleep. There are 15 million Americans of working age livin' with a disability. Companies with a disability inclusion culture were twice as likely to have higher total shareholder returns than their peers.[iii] Disability Hub Europe also backed a study and found that turnover of people with disabilities is 48 percent less than for those without. General staff turnover can be reduced by up to 30 percent when persons with disabilities are included in the workforce. When makin' a purchase decision, 78 percent of people are influenced by whether the company supports access for persons with disabilities. And those who are inclusive of persons with disabilities have a five percent positive impact in reputation. Those who aren't inclusive have a 15 percent negative reputation impact."[iv]

"Wow amazing stats. Turnover is really 48 percent less for people with disabilities?" Jane asked.

"Yupper. You're familiar with Walgreens, the drug store?" Buck asked.

"I am."

"See, Walgreens is a great example of how disability inclusion translates to value. One of their execs, Randy Lewis, started a program to hire people with disabilities. Inspired by his son with autism, Randy wanted to be a leader in disability inclusion. He created a disability employment model in

Walgreens' distribution centers. Walgreens found that people with disabilities perform their jobs just as well as other workers, work more safely, are absent less, and have a lower turnover rate."

"Impressive. Did you say his son is on the autism spectrum?"

"Yup," Buck said. "He was a great sponsor for their disability inclusion initiative because he had firsthand experience with a family member with a disability. Lots of times it takes a loved one with a disability to motivate someone to be passionate about disability inclusion. While he himself didn't have a disability, he saw potential in his own son which pushed him to take action."

"That's good, but are there other companies?" Jade asked.

"Just a who's who of the biggest on earth," Buck said. "AT&T, Amazon, Microsoft, McDonalds, Facebook, Ford, Starbucks, the list goes on and on. Now ya have to ask yourself, why would these companies be spendin' time and money on somethin' if it wasn't worth it? They and many others see the value, enough to make 'em put their money where their mouth is."

"Good point," Jade said.

Buck continued. "Anyways, what you've gotta do is make it clear to your organization that employin' people with disabilities isn't just somethin' you do because you're tryin' to be nice. You're doin' it because there's real value. With one in four people havin' a disability, it's too big a group to ignore.

Any inclusion program worth its salt has disability inclusion as an important piece."

"Gee, when I've thought about inclusion, I've never really considered disability inclusion as a major component. I can see why it needs attention."

"Uh-huh," Buck looked down at his watch. "It's gettin' time for you to be movin' on. But before you go, do you have something to write down?"

Jade took her clipboard and wrote step two:

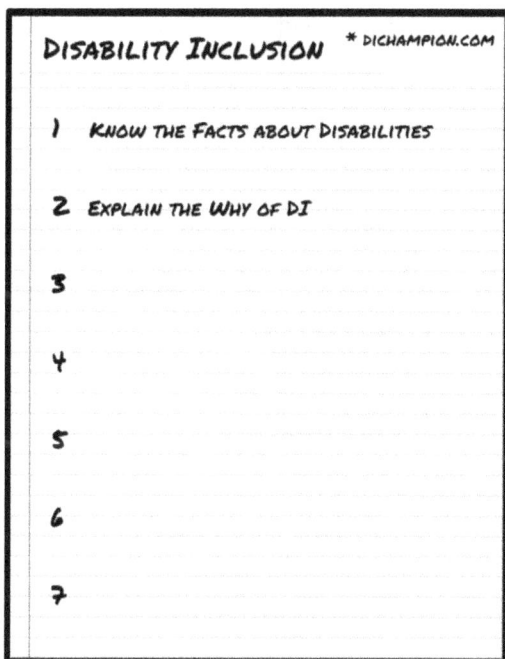

DISABILITY INCLUSION * DICHAMPION.COM

1 KNOW THE FACTS ABOUT DISABILITIES

2 EXPLAIN THE WHY OF DI

3

4

5

6

7

"Dandy. Now before you go, I have somethin' for ya."

"You do?" Jade asked.

"Yup. I just carved it this mornin', 'specially for you. Hope you like it." Buck reached to the table, picked up one of the carvings, and gave it to Jade.

"Why, thank you, Buck."

"Be strong, Jade."

"Thank you." Jade inspected the carving; it was like no carving she'd ever seen.

"Is that who I think it is?" she thought. As she left the room, she turned to see him smiling at her just as the door closed.

"She'll see soon enough," he said to himself as he picked up the carving knife.

Fuhget-About-It

Jade walked into the hallway just as door number 3 opened across the hall to her right. The smell of freshly ground coffee wafted from the room, beckoning for her to come in. *"Bohemian Rhapsody, I love that song,"* she thought as she approached the room. In a corner of the room a barista was grinding coffee beans behind a glass case filled with scones, muffins, and breads. At one of the tables sat a slender woman with brown hair, olive skin, and huge brown eyes. She was hunched over her laptop computer, peering intently into the screen, singing along with Freddie Mercury. A pad of white paper and pen was on the table next to her right hand. She looked up from the screen.

"Jade, I forgot you were coming. So sorry!" the woman said. "I'm Lori. Come sit. Can I get you a latte?"

"Um, sure."

Lori walked over to the barista. "How do you take it?" Lori asked.

"However you do yours is fine."

"OK. Two large lattes; triple shot, no foam, three raw sugars."

"I'll bring them right over, Lori," the barista said.

"Thanks, Lin."

Lori walked back to the table where Jade was sitting.

"I am so happy to be talking with you Jade! How were your first two chats with Anne and Buck?"

"Interesting."

"I love them both, such funny people. Today is 70s day in the café; I love 70s music and anything I can dance to."

"Yeah, every time I get in the car with my dad, he's always got 70s music on." Jade wished she could have pulled the words back after they left her mouth.

"I'm sorry Lori, I didn't mean to offend you."

"Oh please," Lori said as she let out a laugh. "It takes an awful lot to offend me. I'm very comfortable with my age. Fuhget-about-it."

Jade smiled at Lori's Northeast Italian slang.

The barista walked up to the table with two white cups. White foam with a brown heart topped each.

"Enjoy your coffee," the barista said.

"Thanks again, Lin." Lori picked up the cup with both hands, first taking in a deep whiff of the coffee smell, then a big slurp.

"I come here every day for the coffee, it's the best in town."

Jade took a sip. "I usually don't put sugar in my coffee, but this is really good," Jade said.

"Glad you like it." Lori took another sip and put the cup down.

"So, let me tell you a bit about me," Lori started in on her story. "I grew up in Connecticut, the fifth of six kids. I married my high-school sweetheart in 1979. In 1986 we had a daughter, Lindsay. My life was perfect. Then came January 28, 1988. I had just eaten lunch and was talking with my sister-in-law on the phone when I started feeling cold and clammy. Then there was this pain that shot up the back of my neck into my head. I immediately became nauseous. I called my neighbors who both came over; the wife stayed with my daughter while the husband took me to the hospital. My husband met us in the emergency room where we stayed for the next 12 hours. The attending doctor concluded I had a sprained neck and wanted to discharge me. My husband didn't accept the diagnosis. Fortunately, my cousin was the chief of surgery at that hospital, so my husband called him and explained the situation. My cousin dispatched the hospital's best neurosurgeon, who examined me and concluded I had a ruptured brain aneurysm. The neurosurgeon told my husband that they needed to operate immediately to put a drain in my head to remove the pressure on my brain. The doctor prepared my husband for the worst; his wife and the mother of his daughter would likely die in surgery but that it was the only option they had. I was told that before the surgery I was mixing up past and present when I talked; thinking I was in labor with my daughter, speaking in a child's voice, and talking about other events in the past as if they were in the present."

Jade sat on the edge of her seat, captivated by the story. Lori took another sip of latte and continued.

"I ended up having two surgeries; the first to put the drain in my head to relieve the pressure, then a second to repair the rupture. The neurosurgeon, as empathetically as possible, explained the procedures and potential outcomes to my husband and me. Paralysis, not being able to speak, and total memory loss were all possible, assuming I even lived through the surgery, which the doctor said was only a 10 percent chance. I did survive but was left with two long-term side effects: short-term memory loss and occasional issues with balance. I've learned to keep a pad of paper and pen around me at all times, to write down things and not rely on my memory. Ninety percent of those in my situation don't make it; I'll take living with balance and memory loss any day of the week. I'm part of the 10 percent who survive."

Lori paused. "Oh, I love this song!" she said as *Roundabout* began playing. "There's a funny story about this song. When my younger brother was nine, my older brother recorded him singing it while wearing headphones. All you could hear was my brother singing in between all the notes. It was a family joke for years and one my brother never lived down."

Lori took another sip. "Back to business. I learned a lot about brain aneurysms after I recovered. An aneurysm is a weak spot in the wall of a blood vessel that bulges like a bubble.

Brain aneurysms become more common after age 40[v]. I was only 30 when mine ruptured; the doctors suspected that it was the result of a birth defect."

Lori reached into her backpack and grabbed a piece of paper. "I have some statistics I keep handy as I sometimes forget some of them."

Lori looked down at the paper and continued. "One in 50 people have an unruptured brain aneurysm. About 30,000 people in the United States suffer brain aneurysm ruptures each year. Women are 50 percent more likely than men to have brain aneurysms. About 50 percent of all ruptured brain aneurysms are fatal. For those who survive, 66 percent suffer some permanent neurological deficit. And about 15 percent of people with a ruptured aneurysm die before reaching the hospital."[vi]

"So, there's a one in 50 chance I have an unruptured brain aneurysm?" Jade asked.

"Sadly yes. The good news is you'll likely go your entire life without ever knowing it. You may know Neil Young the musician? He had a brain aneurysm which didn't rupture. Sharon Stone the actress also had one but hers ruptured. So did musicians Bret Michaels and Quincy Jones."

"What type of work do you do now?"

"I'm a web developer and social media expert. I have a client base of small businesses that I work with to help them establish and build an online presence. About 15 years after my aneurysm I decided I needed to do something different, so I worked with my younger brother who taught me how to build websites. It's been a challenge for me all these years, particularly with my short-term memory deficit. But I was determined to not let it stop me. And it didn't."

"I'm so impressed, Lori. I know firsthand how taxing your job can be. Congratulations."

Lori smiled. "Very kind of you to say, Jade. Now how about we talk about step three in creating a disability inclusive organization?"

"Sure."

Lori put the paper with statistics back in her backpack. Jade peeked down at Lori's pad of paper on the table and saw "*Jade*" written on it to remind Lori of her name.

"Knowing the facts about disabilities and explaining the why of DI are both super-important steps. I'm sure Anne and Buck did a great job of explaining those to you. Unfortunately, your ability to get the people in the organization to adopt change is likely to fail unless you've got the support of those the organization reports to. You need to ensure that you *get the boss on board* with the disability inclusion initiative."

"Fortunately, Kelly is already on board," Jade said.

"Yes, she is, but her peers and others in the organization may not be. To ensure that all stakeholders are on board and aligned, you need to provide compelling answers to four questions."

As Lori reached into her backpack and pulled out another sheet of paper, Jade looked around the coffee shop, then back at the gold door where she entered the room.

"This place is so weird. A hallway with shiny gold doors, each room different from the last. I wonder what's behind the other doors?"

Just then Jade remembered her thoughts were no different than spoken words. Lori looked up at her and smiled, then looked back down at the paper and started reading to Jade.

"The first question you have to answer is *Why do we need disability inclusion in our organization?'*. In answering this question you need to convincingly articulate that there is a disability inclusion opportunity to be addressed and that there are tangible benefits to seizing the opportunity. The benefits could be something like increased revenue, lower employee turnover, higher employee satisfaction, or positive customer perception. The first question is, in my opinion, the most important. If you don't have a good reason that disability inclusion is needed, then you won't get support for spending time and resources on the initiative. Your answer must be compelling, and the boss needs to agree there is an opportunity to be addressed."

"I've seen this happen in my company," Jade said. "I've watched peers present a great idea for a new feature but not take the time to explain how it would solve a problem. Every time, the feature request was denied because the boss didn't see the problem being solved."

"Same idea," Lori said. "The second question to be answered is *What disability inclusion goals are we striving to achieve?'*

It's great to have an opportunity to address, but there needs to be some type of goal that you are working toward that demonstrates tangible improvement. As an example, one of your goals might be to increase your percentage of employees with disabilities from 10 to 20 percent in the next calendar year. Another might be to reduce overall employee turnover by 50 percent in two years. Whatever the goals, it's important for them to be explicit and, where possible, objectively measurable."

Lori took a sip of her latte. "Mmm, I love this roast. Has a bit of a cocoa taste, don't you think?"

Jade took a sip. "I can taste a hint," she said.

"Good. Now on to question three, *'How do we move forward with a disability inclusion initiative to achieve the goals?'* The answer to this question spells out the plan for how you will execute the initiative. The plan could be as simple as a list of next steps or as formal as a project plan with resources and costs included. It really depends on the organization's project management culture."

"Yes," Jade said. "Our organization is very project management focused, and the project managers love their charts and spreadsheets. I can definitely see us putting more work into a project schedule with resources, costs, milestone checkpoints, risks, issues, and dependencies."

Lori looked down at the paper. "The last question is one that many people either don't ask or are too afraid to ask."

"What's that?" Jade asked.

"It's *What do you need from your boss to be successful?'.* When taking on an initiative like this it's extremely unlikely you will be able to do it on your own. You will need a list of things for your boss to do or provide to help you succeed."

"Like what?"

"It could be things like approval to spend time working on the initiative, budgeted funds, periodic access to the boss for updates, communications that the boss will need to send to the organization showing his or her support for the initiative, or even asking the boss to advocate for the DI initiative with his or her peers or boss. The point is, you need to be clear with what you're asking for and, just as importantly, do it with conviction. The boss is there to help you succeed. If you don't do all you can to help him or her ensure your success, you'll be more likely to fail."

"I've seen that in our organization too," Jade said. "Some of my peers see it as a sign of weakness if they ask for help. Consequently, I've seen them unnecessarily struggle or flat-out fail because they were reluctant to ask for help."

"That's true. I'll put one caveat on the asks for help, though."

"I'm listening," Jade said, ready for the pearl Lori was about deliver.

"Make sure the ask is something either you cannot do yourself or is above your pay grade. For example, sending out an email communication to the organization announcing a disability inclusion initiative would undoubtedly carry more weight if it came from the boss, solely because of her level in the organization. It's not about capability; in fact, you could ghost-write the email and ask her to send it out. It has more impact coming from someone more senior in the organization. It's an unfortunate reality, but what are you gonna do?"

"Good point, Lori."

Lori continued. "If the boss is truly on board, he or she will set the example of the need to create a disability inclusive organization. If the boss is only going through the motions, then it's just a matter of time before the initiative fizzles. Fortunately, Kelly is passionate about disability inclusion. Her leading by example is vital to your success."

Lori took a last sip of her latte. "Now, do you have something you need to write down?" she asked.

Jade took her clipboard and wrote down step three:

DISABILITY INCLUSION * DICHAMPION.COM

1 KNOW THE FACTS ABOUT DISABILITIES

2 EXPLAIN THE WHY OF DI

3 GET THE BOSS ON BOARD

4

5

6

7

"Lori, you are such an inspiration to me. Thank you for the time and your sage advice."

"Thank you, Jade. There's one more thing that might be helpful for you to know. Many people with disabilities don't want to be known as heroes, inspirational, or having superpowers. They just want to be accepted like anyone else. I know you didn't mean anything negative about your inspiration comment, just know that many of us just want to fit into the world."

"I never thought about it that way. Thank you for pointing that out," Jade said.

"No worries, now on to your next appointment."

The two got up from their chairs. Lori walked Jade to the door. "Thank you again, Lori." Jade said.

"You got this, Jade!" Lori said as she hugged Jade.

As Jade turned to leave, she heard *Dancing Queen* playing. She turned to see Lori dancing back to her table.

"How fitting," Jade thought.

Lori looked up at her and smiled as the gold door closed.

Strike Three!

Gold door number 4 opened just as Jade stepped into the hallway. As she walked across the hall to the door, she heard the crack of a bat followed by a man cheering. She looked inside to see a clean-shaven forty-something man with black hair and angular jaw sitting on a lawn chair. He turned around to see Jade standing in the doorway.

"You just missed it! My boy hit a home run!"

"Way to go, Adam!" the man said as the boy trotted around third base on his way to home plate.

"Please come and sit." The man pointed to a lawn chair next to him facing the field. "Let's watch the game while we talk."

Jade walked to the lawn chair, looking around at the baseball diamond, the cheering parents, and the uniformed youngsters on the field.

"This is all so surreal," she said as she sat down in the lawn chair.

"What's surreal?" the man asked.

"What's behind these doors: an office, a log cabin, a coffee shop, and now a baseball field."

"I hope you don't mind being out here while we talk."

Jade looked up at the cloudless sky, enjoying the warmth of the sun on her face. "Not at all," she said.

"Great. My name is Max."

Max reached out to shake Jade's hand. She noticed the slight tremor in his hand as she returned the handshake.

"I'm Jade."

"I've been looking forward to talking, Jade. Can I get you something to drink?"

"I've already had a latte, thank you."

Max smiled. "Ah, that Lori. She sure loves those lattes."

Max reached into the cooler next to him and pulled out a seltzer. The bottle shook in his right hand as he rested it to his chest, put his left over the top and slowly unscrewed the top. Jade noticed the difference in how much more his right hand shook than his left. He put the bottle in his left hand and took a sip.

"So how about I tell you a bit about me?"

"Certainly."

"I'll start at the beginning. I was raised in a poor section of Baltimore, one where many kids didn't even graduate high school, let alone go to college. I was fortunate that I had a couple of outstanding teachers who pushed me to study and get good grades. I decided at an early age that if I wanted more out of life, I had to work for it. I graduated at the top of my high school class and got a scholarship to Notre Dame. It was there I met and married my wife Gail. I graduated with a bachelor's degree in finance and worked at several high-tech companies, working my way up to chief financial officer at a startup. I was 30 when Adam was born. I thought that I had it all--wonderful wife, fantastic job, awesome son. Then on my thirty-fifth birthday I woke up and noticed a twitching in my right index finger. I didn't think much about it at the time. After a few months of the twitching not going away, Gail finally convinced me to go to the doctor to check it out. He told me that it looked like an essential tremor and prescribed a beta blocker. A few months later, my middle and ring finger started twitching. I went back to the doc and he ran more tests on me. I'll never forget that day where Gail, Adam and I sat in his office and he gave me the news. I had Parkinson's disease."

"How old were you again?" Jade asked.

"Thirty-five. Hard to believe; I always thought of Parkinson's as something people older than me got. My first thought was of how Gail and Adam would be affected by living with a husband and father with the condition. Being the analytical person I am, I started learning all I could about Parkinson's. I learned that it occurs when brain cells that make dopamine stop working or die. There's no singular known cause; it could either be genetic or caused from something in the environment. The disease is lifelong and progressive; I'll likely never get better, just worse."

"You'll never get better?" Jade asked.

"Not unless they find a cure. I did the best I could to hide it, the proud person that I am. People at work and our friends started noticing the tremor in my hand as it spread to the rest of my fingers. Then the stiffness started, and it would take longer and longer for me to get in and out of a chair. I thought more and more about my job, my disability, and my need to make life count while I still could. When Gail heard a non-profit organization serving people with disabilities was looking for a CEO, we decided that I should make a career change. My life's mission is now about helping those with disabilities and their loved ones live their lives as fruitfully as possible. I make a lot less than my CFO job, but the work is so much more meaningful. This is where I belong."

"Strike him out, Adam!" Max yelled as Adam took the pitcher's mound.

"How old is Adam," Jade asked.

"He's 12. Hey great pitch, Adam!" Max yelled as the umpire called 'strike three!'

"Sorry about that," Max said. "I just get so into these games."

"No problem, I admire how you support your son."

Max smiled. "Anyway, did you know in the United States there are about a million people living with PD? That's more than the number of people living with multiple sclerosis, muscular dystrophy, and amyotrophic lateral sclerosis, also known as Lou Gehrig's disease, combined. Men are 50 percent more likely to have PD than women. Only four percent of those diagnosed are under the age of 50. And about 60,000 Americans are diagnosed each year."[vii]

"Four percent under age 50. Really." Jade said.

"True. I'm in the distinct minority, having been only 35 when I was diagnosed. On the Hoehn and Yahr scale there are five stages of PD. Stage one is mildest and may manifest itself as tremors on one side of the body. Stage two, which is where I am, includes things like stiffness and tremors on both sides of the body. In stage three, balance becomes an issue; falls become more common. Stage four may mean using a walker or other assistance and living alone is pretty much out of the question. Then there's stage five, where you become a wheelchair user and can't stand on your own. Stages four and five can also include confusion, delusions, and hallucinations.[viii] You might know of some public figures with PD; the most famous probably being Michael J. Fox, who first noticed a pinky twitch when he was 29. Neil Diamond, Ozzy Osbourne, Linda Ronstadt, Muhammad Ali, and Billy Graham all were diagnosed with PD. Being at stage two, I know what my path looks like. I just pray that it progresses slowly enough for me to enjoy life with my family and to help those with disabilities as best I can. There's never a day wasted for me now."

"You have such a good outlook, Max." Jade said.

"Nice job, Adam!" Max said as Adam trotted off the pitcher's mound.

"Sorry again, Jade. Where was I?"

"Never a wasted day for you."

"Oh right. Even though today I don't take a day for granted, it wasn't always the case. I did a lot of wallowing in self-pity. I also know that those with PD can be more susceptible to depression. My job now is to have as good an outlook on life as possible and take care of myself as best I can. Gail is my rock; I honestly don't know what I would do without her. Yes, there are struggles, but we all agree we need to meet them head on."

Max took another sip. "I can tell my voice is getting more hoarse. Another symptom of PD."

"It's OK, you can stop anytime you need," Jade said.

"I'm good, besides this is important stuff. So, I guess you'd like to know what the fourth step is in creating a disability inclusive organization, huh?"

"That would be great."

"Good. So by now you've picked up on knowing the facts about DI, explaining why DI is important, and ensuring the boss is on board. Those are important steps to paint a clear picture of what a disability inclusive organization needs to look like. Knowing where you need to be is crucial, but unless you know your starting point, you're likely to waste a lot of time and resources along the way. You need to *assess the DI current state.*"

"In software engineering we refer to something called the 'as-is' where you document how something works today as a basis for improving through technology. Same thing?" Jade asked.

"Precisely," Max said. "In understanding the DI current state you document the environment as it is today, so you know where to focus to get to your destination. Lori probably talked with you about setting goals. Understanding your current state helps you understand the starting point for the measures that gauge DI success."

"Yes she did," Jade said.

"Good. Now let's talk about what I think a good current state analysis includes. There are five dimensions: people, processes, technology, ecosystem, and infrastructure."

Max stopped for a minute to take a long drink. "Let's go through each one. In the people dimension, you want to understand things like the current inclusion makeup of the people in your organization, the inclusiveness of job requirements, and what people value. In reviewing processes, documenting things like how candidates are interviewed and hired, how employees are onboarded, and how people get rewarded and promoted are important. With technology, you analyze things like how assistive technologies are or are not being made available to those who need them, and how existing systems may be limiting to someone with a disability. When looking at the ecosystem you need a clear picture of what to expect from suppliers, what customers expect from you, and what competitors and peer companies are doing. Then with infrastructure, you understand how your facility may enhance or inhibit someone with a disability from performing a job. I'm just scratching the surface here with what needs to be looked at, and the areas of examination could vary depending on the organization and environment. The key takeaway is that a good current state analysis looks at all five dimensions: people, processes, technology, ecosystem, and infrastructure."

"Yup, I'm familiar with these dimensions as a systems engineer," Jade said. "It helps me that you use this terminology when talking about a DI initiative."

"Great, Jade. Do you have your clipboard?"

Jade took out her clipboard and wrote down step four:

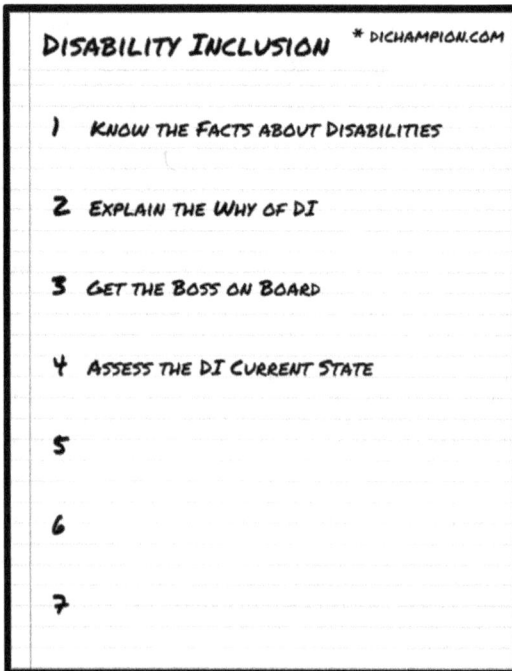

DISABILITY INCLUSION   * DICHAMPION.COM

1   KNOW THE FACTS ABOUT DISABILITIES

2   EXPLAIN THE WHY OF DI

3   GET THE BOSS ON BOARD

4   ASSESS THE DI CURRENT STATE

5

6

7

"Max, I admire your priorities and how you changed your career path to help others with disabilities. Gives me a lot to think about."

"You may be faced with a similar choice someday, Jade."

"Um, OK. Thank you, Max." Jade was a bit taken aback by Max's comment.

"I have faith in you, Jade. You take care of yourself." He slowly stood up from the lawn chair, letting out a grunt as he straightened into a standing position. He reached out his hand to shake hers, the tremor even more visible to her. She shook it as if she didn't notice.

"Goodbye, Max." Jade turned and walked off the field out the gold door. Just as door number 5 opened, she heard a synthesized voice say, *"That you, Jade?"* coming from inside.

R-E-S-P-E-C-T

Jade slowly walked toward the door, not expecting to hear what sounded like a computer with a female voice talking to her. She looked in the room to see an Asian woman sitting in a motorized wheelchair. She was on a pier looking out over a lake, the reflection of the sun dancing on the water as it was about to set. In front of her at chest height was what looked like a computer tablet mounted to the wheelchair. Her left hand rested on a joystick which started moving as Jade entered the room.

"Nice to meet you, Jade!" the female voice said. "I'm Peg. Please enjoy this beautiful sunset with me!"

"I'd love to!" Jade stood next to Peg, both facing the orange hue of the setting sun.

"I love being out here. The cool evening air and smell of the water make me feel so good. Do you want to hear a joke?" Peg asked.

"Uh, sure."

"What did the turkey say to the turkey hunter?"

"I don't know, what did the turkey say to the turkey hunter?"

Jade watched Peg's eyes appear to smile as she moved the joystick.

"Quack! Quack!"

"Uhhhh!" Jade groaned.

"I love corny dad jokes!"

Jade smiled. "My dad told jokes like this all the time. I have to admit they still crack me up."

"Me too. How is your visit?"

"Honestly, it's like nothing I've ever experienced. I still don't know where I am, how I got here, or how I get back home."

"Trust me, Jade. It will all make sense soon. You may notice it takes me a bit more time for me to say things. I have to communicate through what is called an augmented and alternative communication, or AAC, device. This device uses a keyboard as well as an easy communicator, or ECO application. The ECO has 144 icons per page which allow me to say things by pointing to the icon. Watch this."

Peg moved the joystick. An arrow on the screen moved from icon to icon.

"You are almost as pretty as me!"

Jade laughed. "You're a sassy one!" she said.

"Yes I am. You see my joystick?"

"Yes."

"AAC devices accept a number of different input forms. A user can press the screen, use a joystick like I do, or even control it using their eyes. You know the cosmologist Stephen

Hawking? He used an AAC that he operated through eye gaze. Some people like using the icons, but I prefer to spell everything out."

"I've never seen anyone use an AAC. Fascinating."

"It gives me so much freedom to communicate. Aside from speech I type emails, browse the internet, do just about everything a regular computer does. Now how about more about me?"

"Sure." While Peg talked, Jade kept looking at her eyes. Each time Peg's synthetic voice talked Peg's eyes seemed to underscore the emotion that the mechanical voice couldn't communicate on its own.

"When I was 11 months old, I was diagnosed with Cerebral Palsy, which is caused by abnormal brain development or damage which affects a person's ability to control his or her muscles. There are three main types of CP: spastic, dyskinetic, and ataxic. Spastic is the most common, occurring in 80 percent of people with CP. They have increased muscle tone which makes their muscles stiff. People with dyskinetic CP have uncontrollable hand, arm, foot, and leg movements, and can also have difficulty sucking, swallowing, or talking. People with ataxic CP have problems with balance and coordination. There can also be a mix of CP types, the most common being spastic dyskinetic CP[ix]. I have spastic CP. As I got older my muscles became tighter. I require a full-time caregiver; my mom has been that person my entire life."

"Peg, are you OK with me asking questions? I don't want to offend you in any way."

"Fire away, second most pretty person." Jade watched Peg's eyes laugh as she joked.

"Have you been in a wheelchair your entire life?"

"Yes, even though my muscles became tighter as I got older, I still was never able to walk on my own." Peg turned her head and took a sip of water from a straw that led into a container fastened to her wheelchair.

"Growing up, I kept telling people that I wanted to go to college, but pretty much everyone around me thought I would never be able to go, let alone graduate. My teachers didn't evaluate me based on my knowledge, they assumed that I was not able to learn like the other students due to my disability. I really wanted to show them that I could get a higher education and be successful. Well guess what? I now have a master's degree in social work and work for a non-profit that assists people with disabilities. I was excited to get letters after my name; I did it because I wanted others to realize that anyone can do whatever they want to, and they have a right to do so. Graduating from college was one of the best things that has ever happened to me. I proved them all wrong. Yay me!"

"Yes, yay you!" Jade said.

"I want to tell you more about CP. About 764,000 people in the U.S. have at least one CP symptom. Ten thousand babies are born each year with CP. It occurs 35 percent more in boys than girls. And 41 percent of children with CP also have some type of cognitive disorder like autism.[x] And here's the one statistic I really like: six out of 10 people with CP have normal or superior intelligence.[xi] I may move and communicate differently, but I'm still smart as a whip."

Peg took another sip from the straw. "So how about we talk about step five in creating a disability inclusive organization?"

"That would be great." Jade had totally forgotten that the voice she was hearing was synthetic. The words and emotions were all Peg.

"This step can actually happen at the same time as assessing the DI current state; in fact, it's better if it does. Trying to create a DI organization can be a hard job, one that you won't be able to do on your own. Even if your boss is a strong advocate, you won't be successful on your own. You will need other people in the organization who are respected by their peers to be part of your mission. You will need to *assemble your DI influencers.*"

Jade listened attentively, keeping her gaze into Peg's eyes, amazed that all of Peg's words were created through her moving a joystick.

"In assembling your team you'll need to make sure the team has several qualities. The first that I already mentioned is they need to be respected by others. No one is going to listen to someone who can't command respect. Second, they will need to be passionate about disability inclusion; and some of them need to be people who have a disability. Third, they will need to commit to work on the initiative and not have it get put on the back burner."

"I get the back-burner thing," Jade said. "We've had some initiatives at work where some people get all excited about working on it only to have their excitement fizzle over time."

"Yes. They need to be committed. In fact, their direct manager needs to be committed as well. No management support means that over time, other things will take higher priority. And your DI initiative will slowly die."

"Now once you have your DI influencers, you'll need to prepare them with facts and stats just like you did with the boss. This step is particularly important. If your influencers aren't armed with information, then their ability to influence others becomes more difficult. It's not enough to be passionate; they have to have the data to complement the passion."

"Yup, makes sense. I tend to listen to someone who can articulate their message with passion using facts and stats to back it up." Jade said.

"Good. Next, your influencers should serve as your listening system to challenges being expressed in the organization. For instance, someone may express concern about how to handle team activities when a team member has limited mobility. Hearing concerns like this help you and your influencers design training and other communications to address top-of-mind issues. This brings up another important character trait of your influencers. They need to be empathetic listeners who aren't dismissive of input received. Anything said to them needs to be treated with respect. R-E-S-P-E-C-T. I'd sing it but there's no Aretha Franklin voice on my AAC."

"Nicely done," Jade said. "That song will be going through my head the rest of the day."

"Yes, I love that song. Now the last thing I will leave you with is that it's always preferable if the person leading the DI initiative has a disability. It's not that someone without a disability can't do it, but it's good if he or she does have one."

"I hope I'm able to do it without a disability," Jade said.

Peg was silent for a moment; Jade couldn't help but notice the change in Peg's normally smiling eyes.

Peg resumed her joystick movements. "Do you have something you need to write down?"

"Yes." Jade took her clipboard out and wrote step five:

DISABILITY INCLUSION   * DICHAMPION.COM

1   KNOW THE FACTS ABOUT DISABILITIES

2   EXPLAIN THE WHY OF DI

3   GET THE BOSS ON BOARD

4   ASSESS THE DI CURRENT STATE

5   ASSEMBLE YOUR DI INFLUENCERS

6

7

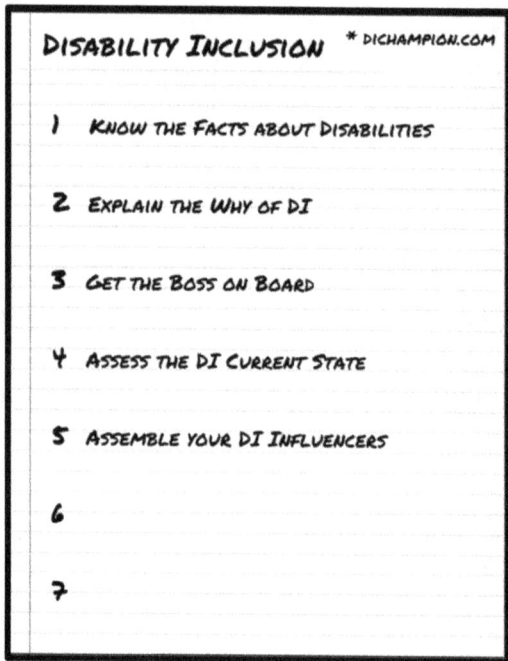

"Peg, it was so much fun talking with you," Jade said.

"Yes it was," Peg said. "Be successful, second prettiest girl!"

"I will, thank you." Jade turned and walked up the pier toward the gold door. She turned back to see Peg and her wheelchair's silhouette against the dark orange horizon.

Kale Smoothie

Door number 6 opened just as Jade walked into the hallway. Inside was a desk with a large computer screen mounted on a bracket attached to the desk. A woman peered out from the side of the screen.

"Hello, Jade."

"Hello."

"I'm Deb. Come on around and grab a chair."

Jade walked behind the desk just as Deb stood to greet her.

"It's a pleasure meeting you, Jade," Deb said as she reached out her hand.

"Likewise."

"I just made myself a kale smoothie. Would you like one?"

"Something healthy to drink. That would be great."

Deb got out two glasses and poured the green drink. "I'm trying a new recipe; kale with avocado and orange. Let me know what you think."

"Funny, that's my go-to," Jade said as she took a sip. "Terrific."

"Thanks."

Jade noticed a bike just like hers by the door. "You ride?"

"About 50 miles a day," Deb said. "I'm entering my first triathlon later this year. Biking is my strong suit. I'm not so good at swimming and running. It's always been a personal goal of mine to run a triathlon. There's no way I'll win; my goal is just to finish."

"I admire that," Jade said. "I love biking too but never liked running or swimming much. I love your attitude. Just finish."

Deb took a sip of the smoothie. "Mmm, that is good. The orange really adds some zing to it."

Deb put her glass down. "Let me tell you a bit about me. When I was 10 years old, I was ice skating with my parents when I slipped on the ice and fell right on my head. I was in a coma for a week and ended up with something called cortical visual impairment. The parts of my brain that receive visual stimuli from my eyes sustained enough damage that my eyesight was affected. Ever since then I've been visually impaired."

"So, are you blind?" Jade asked.

"Not exactly. Let me tell you a bit about visual impairment. First you need to understand how vision is measured. You're familiar with the term 20/20 vision, right?"

"Yes."

"Good. The number is a measure of visual acuity, which refers to how close a person needs to be to an object that's 20 feet away to see it in detail. Someone with 20/20 vision can see something 20 feet away at good detail. Two of the most popular eye charts which measure visual acuity are the Snellen chart, which is the chart with different letters, and the Tumbling E chart, which is the capital letter E flipped upside down, right side up, and on each side. Each line on the chart represents a measure of acuity at 20 feet. For example, on the Snellen chart if you could only read the top letter E at 20 feet and nothing below, then your vision would be 20/200, which means that your vision at 20 feet is the same as what someone with 20/20 vision could see at 200 feet. Each successive line on the chart represents a visual acuity measurement, with the eighth line representing 20/20 visual acuity."

"It's funny how even though I've heard 20/20 for years I never knew what it meant," Jade said.

"You're not alone," Deb said. "Now let's talk about visual field. Visual field is the total area a person can see without moving the eyes from side to side. For someone with no visual field deficit, their horizontal field in one eye is about 95 degrees and vertical is between 60 and 75 degrees. Good so far?"

"I think so."

"Good. Let's apply it to what is considered legal blindness. Someone is considered legally blind if he or she meets either of the following: they have a visual acuity of 20/200 or less in their better seeing eye with conventional correction, like prescription glasses or contact lenses, or if their visual field is 20 degrees or less. That's commonly referred to as tunnel vision."

"Twenty degrees isn't very much," Jade said.

"No, it's not. In addition to legal blindness, there are two other visual impairment categories. The first is low vision, which is what I have. This is where visual acuity is 20/70 or poorer in the better seeing eye and cannot be corrected with prescription glasses or contact lenses. The other is total blindness, which is a complete lack of light and form perception. While this is what people typically think when they hear the term 'blind,' only 15 percent of those with a sight disorder are totally blind.[xii] There are some other interesting statistics. 2.4 percent of Americans age 16 and up are sight impaired. Three percent of African Americans, 2.4 percent white, 2.2 percent Hispanic, 1.4 percent Asian, and 3.8 percent American Indian or Alaska Native are sight impaired. Of those who are sight impaired, only 15.7 percent attain a bachelor's degree or higher. Only 29.5 percent of those who are of working age and not institutionalized work full-time. That means over 70 percent of those who are sight impaired and able to work are not employed full-time."[xiii]

Deb took a long drink of her smoothie and continued. "Now, as for me being low-vision, I use a few tools which help me do my job. I use a larger monitor with a larger font size. I also use an electronic magnifier if I need to read something in hard copy. What I really love is these bioptic telescopic glasses." Deb pulled a pair of glasses from her purse. At the top half of each lens was what looked like a miniature monocular.

"These little babies are quite literally my license to drive. The bottom half of the lenses are just typical prescription eyeglasses. However, when I tilt my head down and look through the telescopic lenses, I see well enough to get behind the wheel. They've made a huge difference in my quality of life. In fact, after my accident my parents wouldn't let me feel sorry for myself or talk myself out of doing things because of my disability. I've become a very determined woman who gets things done. I have a master's degree in project management and work for an internet start-up. My colleagues call me 'No Drama Deb' because I know how to execute calmly and deliberately while everyone else is freaking out."

"No Drama Deb," Jade laughed at the nickname. "We could certainly use you at my company. We have a lot of people who run around with their hair on fire as soon as something goes wrong."

"I know the type." Deb put the glasses down on her desk.

"Now, how about I tell you about the sixth step in creating a disability inclusive organization? As a project manager, this one is the most fun for me. In the previous steps you set your goals and assessed your DI current state. You know where you're starting from, and you know where you want to end up. Now it's about figuring out how you get from point A to point B in such a way that you instill new habits and philosophies in the organization so they simply become part of what gets done. It's about *driving the DI DNA change plan.*"

"DNA, interesting word choice," Jade said.

69

"It is. You may also think about it as changing the DI culture. Every organization has a type of culture that is typically set by its leadership. If a leader is a full-steam-ahead type of leader, then the rest of the organization will tend to inherit that trait as part of its DNA. This is why it's so crucial to ensure your boss is on board with the DI initiative. An organization's DNA is a reflection of its leadership."

Deb took a sip of smoothie. "You may remember in *assessing the current DI state* how Max talked about people, processes, technology, infrastructure and ecosystem?"

"Sure do."

"Good. In executing your DI DNA change plan it's important to look at each of these aspects of the organization and determine what needs to change to achieve your goals. Depending on your starting point, some of the things I'm going to talk about may be more or less important for your organization, so you'll need to decide where to focus. When you think about people, consider things like job requirement changes, education and training needs for both managers and individual contributors, the metrics used, and how rewards and recognition are given. Also key to your change plan is how things are communicated across the organization, which underscores the importance of having a good communication plan. You want to be able to explain who gets communicated to, what gets communicated, its frequency, and how it's communicated, such as email, training class, or executive briefing. Make sense so far?"

"Yes, it's just so much to take in," Jade said.

"Don't worry, you'll be able to go to *DIchampion.com* later for the details."

"Right, I almost forgot."

"Now, with processes, you'll want to consider what needs to change with things like how candidates are interviewed and onboarded to ensure the organization accommodates people with disabilities. In the technology area, look at what assistive technologies and systems changes need to be implemented. With infrastructure, you'll need to make accommodating facility, workstation, and other environmental changes. Then comes the ecosystem. There may be changes you'll make in how you choose and work with suppliers, how you communicate with customers so they are aware of your new DI DNA, how you work with peer companies to compare notes on DI, and how your DI DNA program sets you apart from competitors."

Deb took another sip and continued. "As any good project manager knows, there are usually more things to do than hours in the day. In my job it's all about making choices--choosing those things to do that are most important and prioritizing them over those which are less important, not critical, or have a lower value back to the organization. This is where a strong project manager is paramount to a successful DI DNA change plan. The project manager doesn't have to be the initiative owner; in fact, I like it when the project manager and initiative owner are two separate people. The initiative owner can focus on ensuring the right things get done to change the organization's DI DNA, and the project manager focuses on the resources needed to execute the plan on time and within budget. For example, the person who designed my bike is not the same person who manufactured it. Same concept applies to your DI DNA change plan."

"I understand," Jade said. "My peer at work is a product manager who decides on the best features to include in our software. My job is to put them in and ensure they work to the product manager's specifications."

"Yes, same idea. Now there's one more concept I want to talk about. In your DI DNA change plan, you are working to get people in the organization to embrace a new way of doing things. With any change plan you have one of four outcomes: resistance, which means 'we don't want it,' ambivalence, which means 'we're OK either way,' acceptance, which means 'we want it,' and embracing, which means 'we need it.' Your job is to get the organization to embrace the change--anything else and your initiative is more likely to fail."

"That's a good way to put it," Jade said. "I want people to feel they were missing out on something if we weren't a disability inclusive organization."

"Right. Now do you have something you want to write down?"

"Yes." Jade took out her clipboard. "Drive the DI DNA Change Plan," she said as she wrote. *"Can't forget about*

DIchampion.com." she thought as she underlined it at the page's top right:

DISABILITY INCLUSION * DICHAMPION.COM

1 KNOW THE FACTS ABOUT DISABILITIES

2 EXPLAIN THE WHY OF DI

3 GET THE BOSS ON BOARD

4 ASSESS THE DI CURRENT STATE

5 ASSEMBLE YOUR DI INFLUENCERS

6 DRIVE THE DI DNA CHANGE PLAN

7

"Thank you for the time, Deb, and good luck in the triathlon." Just then Jade remembered something. "Oh my gosh! I forgot my bike helmet back in Anne's office!"

"Don't worry Jade, you'll get it back soon enough."

"I'll go get it now. Take care Deb."

"Execute well," Deb said as she turned back to her screen.

Jade walked out of the room and just as she was about to turn left to go back to Anne's door, she heard door number 7 open, and looked down the hallway to her right.

"Hurry up, I don't have all day!" the man's voice said.

Peanut Shells

Jade looked into the room behind door number 7.

"I'm just going to get my helmet." Jade said.

"Get it later! You're wasting my time!"

"Uh, OK." Jade was taken aback by his aggressive demeanor; so different from the other six. She entered the room, hearing the crunch of peanut shells as she took each step. The room was sparsely lit and reeked of cigarette smoke. At the back of the room was a wood-paneled bar where a bartender stood in front of shelves lined with liquor bottles. The only other person in the room was a man with long scraggly hair and a bushy beard. He sat in a worn-out wheelchair at a round table, eating a burger and fries.

"Sit." The man in the wheelchair motioned to a wooden chair across the table from him.

Jade tentatively sat down, the chair wobbling as she tried to get comfortable. "What's your name?"

"Captain Mark Espinoza. Call me Captain."

"OK, Captain." Jade would have preferred to call him Mark but didn't want to further agitate him.

"Let's get this over with," Mark said. "Your name is Jade, right?"

"Yes."

"Jade, do you know why you're here?"

"Um, based on my prior meetings it's to learn about how to create a disability inclusive organization."

"Try again."

Jade gave him a puzzled look. "Excuse me?"

"Try again!"

Jade shuffled on the chair to try to get comfortable. "To promote disability inclusion with my team," she said, hoping it was the answer he was looking for.

"Wrong again."

Jade was exasperated. "What's the right answer then, Captain?" she asked.

"Closing time in ten, Mark," the bartender said as he cleaned the bar.

"I can read the clock, 'tender!" Mark yelled at the bartender.

"Sheesh, take it easy already," the bartender said.

Mark turned his attention back to Jade. "First, about me. I went into the army straight out of high school, wanted to defend my country, you know, baloney like that. Did three tours of duty in Afghanistan. Just as I was about to go home at the end of the third tour, I took a bullet in the spine at C5 around chest level while I was changing clothes so didn't have my body armor on. Was going to come back home and marry my high-school sweetheart and work with my dad in the construction business. Returned in a wheelchair. Dad put me to work shuffling papers, but the job just wasn't me. My fiancé couldn't handle my being in a wheelchair so she left me. I've tried some odd jobs but nothing seemed to work out. I got this gig talking to people like you only because I had to do it, not because I wanted to be here. Not your warm fuzzy story like you've been hearing from the others, is it?"

"No, it isn't, Captain."

"You're darn right it isn't. I wasn't embraced or even accepted when I came back. People looked at me and labeled me as incapable, not able to add value, not someone who had something to say. You heard a lot of success stories today about how people with disabilities are embraced and valued. I'm not one of them."

"I'm sorry all this happened to you, Captain."

"Yeah, so am I. You know who my childhood hero was? Christopher Reeve. I loved him in the Superman movies. Then in 1995 he was thrown from a horse and landed on his head. Fractured the top two vertebrae in his neck. Paralyzed him from the neck down. Even needed a respirator to help him breathe. He became a strong advocate for those with paralysis. After I was injured, I looked to him for inspiration, so I could come back and live a fruitful life. Even studied up on different types of paralysis to maybe be someone who could help others. What I have is paraplegia, which is paralysis from the waist down. Reeve had quadriplegia, which is when all four limbs are paralyzed, and sometimes organ function is impacted. Hemiplegia is paralysis on one side of the body, typically caused by stroke. Diplegia affects the same area on both sides of the body, like arms or face. Monoplegia affects just one limb. Then there's something called locked-in syndrome, where the only thing a person can move is his or her eyes. Paralysis could be periodic, which is often triggered by something a person eats. There's sleep paralysis, which happens while you're waking up or falling asleep. Bell's palsy makes half of your face appear to droop. Todd's paralysis is triggered by a seizure in someone with epilepsy. And tick paralysis is caused by neurotoxins in some ticks."[xiv]

Mark grabbed a cold soggy French fry, soaked it in ketchup and popped it in his mouth.

"The Christopher and Dana Reeve Foundation conducted a study about paralysis. They found that 1.7 percent of the U.S. population lives with some form of paralysis. One third were paralyzed due to strokes, with 27 percent due to spinal cord injuries and 18 percent from multiple sclerosis. Seventeen percent served in the military, with 40 percent of those saying their injury occurred while on active duty. When it comes to employment, only 15 percent of those living with paralysis have a job."[xv]

"Fifteen percent?" Jade asked.

"Fifteen. I'm considered lucky to have a job despite hating it. Musician Teddy Pendergrass and baseball player Roy Campanella were paralyzed in car accidents. Franklin Delano

Roosevelt was paralyzed by what was thought to be polio. The athlete Mike Utley was paralyzed while playing in a football game. And musician Curtis Mayfield was paralyzed after stage lighting fell on him during a concert."

Jade's chair creaked as she shifted her weight to try to get comfortable.

"Not very comfy, huh?" Mark said.

"Not really."

"Poor thing. I'd give my right arm to be uncomfortable in a chair like that." Mark put his head down, reflecting on his own words. Jade looked at him as he sat, feeling bad for the man whose anger masked profound sadness.

Mark lifted his head and continued. "Now for step seven. No Drama Deb talked with you about driving the DI DNA change plan, right?"

"She did."

"Did she tell you what happens after the DI goals are met?"

"Not really."

"You're an engineer, right?"

"Yes."

"What happens after you finish a project?"

Jade paused before answering. "I move on to the next project."

"Exactly the problem!"

"What? My to-do list is a mile long, I need to work the next project."

"Pffttt. Changing the DI DNA isn't about just stopping work and hoping the changes stick. Hitting goals is just the start of the journey. You've got to *keep the DI momentum going.*"

"How do I do that?" Jade asked.

"There are five things you need to do to keep the momentum going," he said as he thrust five calloused fingers at Jade's face.

"First, your metrics are your ammunition. Keep measuring your results and reporting them. People are motivated by what's measured on their DI report card. For example, if hiring and retention metrics for people with disabilities is not included in a manager's performance appraisal then the manager won't focus on it because he or she isn't rewarded for good performance."

"I understand. When I set my objectives at the beginning of the year, I focus on those objectives and the measures which demonstrate success." Jade said.

"Yes," Mark said. "Second is to continue assessing what is happening in the area of disability inclusion with providers, peer companies, suppliers, customers, and competitors and adjust your DI program accordingly. For example, if there are new technologies that assist those with a specific disability, are those technologies applicable in your organization? Or if a disability inclusion provider develops new training for managers who lead people with disabilities, would that training be helpful to managers in your organization? You don't want your DI program to get outdated because no one is charged with ensuring your tools are the most applicable at the time."

"I can see that. If we don't use the latest computers or programming languages, we won't be competitive," Jade said.

"Right. The third thing is to continue assessing employee perceptions about how good the organization is doing with disability inclusion. Questions about disability inclusion should be embedded in employee satisfaction surveys and the survey results reported to the person heading up the disability inclusion initiative. Sagging disability inclusion employee satisfaction should be treated as a management issue with corrective actions put in place to increase employee DI satisfaction. Make sense?"

"It does," Jade said.

"Good. The fourth thing is to communicate the progress and results to the rest of the organization using your communication plan developed in step six. It's not just about the good stuff; if something needs to improve, that should be communicated too. You don't want to be accused of spouting propaganda that tarnishes your credibility."

"Credibly communicate progress and results. Got it."

"Now the fifth thing is the hardest for some. You need to continue to hold the boss accountable for walking the DI talk and make sure the boss holds others in the organization accountable. As you've probably heard before, an organization's beliefs and priorities are a reflection of what the leader believes and thinks is important. If your boss all of a sudden telegraphs that DI is no longer a priority, then the rest of the organization will follow suit. You need to be the conscience of the organization and have a good enough relationship with the boss to remind him or her of DI's importance."

"I don't think Kelly will do that," Jade said.

"Maybe not intentionally, but remember, leaders have a lengthy list of issues they juggle. It's easy to forget about something that may be important but not urgent. Your job is to ensure that DI doesn't get crowded out by those things that might be urgent."

"I see," Jade said. "I tend to let urgent things continue to push important but not urgent things to the bottom of my to-do list. I went to a leadership class where we talked a lot about making time for those things that are important but not urgent. I'm still working on building this leadership muscle."

Mark ate another soggy fry and continued. "When we first met, I asked you if you knew why you were here. I admit it was a bit of a trick question. Yes, you will be creating an organization that is inclusive of disabilities, but for you it's much deeper. After you leave me, you're going to understand much better why you're here, and it will change you forever."

Jade was shaken by this ominous warning. "What do you mean?" She said.

"Do you have something to write down?" Mark asked.

Jade took her clipboard and wrote down step seven. She wrote tentatively, unnerved by Mark's comment:

DISABILITY INCLUSION   * DICHAMPION.COM

1 KNOW THE FACTS ABOUT DISABILITIES

2 EXPLAIN THE WHY OF DI

3 GET THE BOSS ON BOARD

4 ASSESS THE DI CURRENT STATE

5 ASSEMBLE YOUR DI INFLUENCERS

6 DRIVE THE DI DNA CHANGE PLAN

7 KEEP THE DI MOMENTUM GOING

"It's time for you to go, Jade. I'm relying on you to help people like me not be treated the way I've been treated. I'm counting on you, Jade."

"Very well, Captain." Jade got up from the table and slowly walked toward the door, the crunch of the peanut shells breaking the silence as she stepped. The gold door slammed shut behind her as she left the room, startling her. She looked up the hallway to the white wall at the end, and the six gold doors, three on either side. The hallway then got hazy, as if looking through a telescope going out of focus.

"Jade, can you hear me?"

Sport

The haze had thickened to a pea-soup fog, then as it started clearing, Jade saw a woman in a white coat standing above her.

"Jade, can you hear me?" the woman said again over a steady blip sound.

The woman's face came into focus. "Who are you?" Jade asked.

"I'm Dr. Nguyen. Do you know where you are?"

"No."

"You're at St. Vincent's Hospital intensive care. We're going to take good care of you."

Jade tried to lift her arms. Every inch of her head, chest and arms hurt. Even talking was painful.

"What happened?" Jade muttered.

"You were hit by a bus riding home from work." Just then she felt someone grab her right hand.

"How you feeling, sport?"

Jade recognized the voice. "Dad?"

"Yup." She turned her head to see him standing over her, his eyes welled with tears.

"You're my strong girl; we thought we were going to lose you there for a bit," he said, a tear running down his cheek. He leaned down to her hand and kissed it. "Mom is on her way; she just went home to shower."

"What day is it?" she asked.

"Friday."

"The accident happened on Tuesday?"

"Three weeks ago Tuesday." He said.

"I've been out for over three weeks?"

"We're just so thankful you're with us," he said, his voice crackling.

"How come my legs don't hurt?"

Dad put his head back on her hand.

"What's going on?" Jade asked Dr. Nguyen.

"Jade, when the bus hit you it fractured your C5 vertebrae and damaged your spinal cord. We're doing all we can to help you."

"Am I paralyzed?"

"Yes. From the waist down."

For the first time in her life Jade heard her father cry as Dr. Nguyen said the words. Jade slowly closed her eyes, unable to process what she just heard.

The Card

Jade rode the bus from her apartment to her first day back at work. The nine months since the accident were a tangled mass of emotions, physical therapy, and learning how to live independently as a wheelchair user. She had to move from her apartment in the city to her parents' home in the suburbs, both because she needed extra help and it was now impossible to go up or down the stairs at her apartment. Seeing friends and family members was difficult at first, mostly because they didn't know what to say or how to act around her. She was grateful for anyone who reached out to her with a word of encouragement or a shoulder to cry on, but she was also disappointed in those who didn't call, visit, or text. She became determined to live independently and not let her paraplegia limit who she was as a person.

As her bus got closer to her office, she felt nervous anticipation. It was the first time many of her colleagues would see her as a wheelchair user. She left the bus and wheeled up to the front door, then into the lobby and up the elevator. When the elevator opened on her floor, she was greeted to a WELCOME BACK JADE! sign hanging in the lobby. She wheeled through the lobby into the work area. Coworkers, even those who didn't know her well before the accident, welcomed her with fist bumps and moving words. She came up to her cubicle which was filled with cards, flowers, and gifts. Waiting there was Kelly.

"Welcome back Jade! We missed you so much!" Kelly said.

"Thank you, Kelly."

"Look, just take things easy for a few days. Give yourself some time to get back in the swing. Let me know if you need anything at all."

"That's so kind of you Kelly, thank you."

"Besides, you've got a lot of cards and gifts to open!"

"That I do."

"We'll talk later." Kelly gave Jade a gentle pat on her shoulder and went back to her office. Jade wheeled into her cubicle and started to work on opening the cards and gifts. Just as she reached for the last box, she noticed the strange wrapping. She looked closer at the paper and recognized the pattern; a patchwork of gold doors randomly numbered 1 through 7. She carefully unwrapped the paper to not rip it, then opened the box.

"Oh my gosh!" she said. She reached in and pulled out the clipboard with the seven steps:

DISABILITY INCLUSION   * DICHAMPION.COM

1 KNOW THE FACTS ABOUT DISABILITIES

2 EXPLAIN THE WHY OF DI

3 GET THE BOSS ON BOARD

4 ASSESS THE DI CURRENT STATE

5 ASSEMBLE YOUR DI INFLUENCERS

6 DRIVE THE DI DNA CHANGE PLAN

7 KEEP THE DI MOMENTUM GOING

She then pulled out the bike helmet she left in Anne's office, then the carving Buck gave her--a woman who looked just like her sitting in a wheelchair. She didn't understand at the time why Buck gave her the unusual carving; now it made perfect sense. She looked back in the box and saw an envelope. She opened it and pulled out a card with an embossed gold door on the front. She slowly ran her fingers over the door, feeling the raised outline of the door panels and the gold ring knocker at the center.

She flipped open the card and read:

Good luck – Anne
Be strong – Buck
You got this! – Lori
I have faith in you – Max
Be successful second prettiest girl! – Peg
Execute well – No Drama Deb
I'm counting on you – Captain Mark

As she read each name, she thought about each of the seven. Anne's ability to recount fact after fact. Buck's easy-going style. Lori's love of music. Max's courageous career choices. Peg's sense of humor. Deb's calm, deliberate demeanor. And Captain Mark's sadness masked in anger and frustration. Then she thought about Mark's question to her, *"Why are you here?"* In the nine months since the accident she didn't really give it much thought, but seeing the card, clipboard, carving, and helmet made it all clear. She grabbed the clipboard and noticed there was a second sheet behind the first with only the words *Why am I here?* written across the top. She paused for a moment then wrote:

WHY AM I HERE?

I AM HERE TO BE A
FIERCE ADVOCATE TO
ENSURE EVERY PERSON
WITH A DISABILITY IS
TREATED FAIRLY AND IS
GIVEN AN OPPORTUNITY TO
CONTRIBUTE TO HIS OR
HER MAXIMUM POTENTIAL.

She tacked the pages with the seven steps and the *Why am I here?* statement on the wall in her cubicle. She sat there for a few minutes, just staring at the two pieces of paper. *"I know what I need to do,"* she thought to herself. She backed out of her cubicle then wheeled over to Kelly's office.

"What can I do for you Jade?" Kelly asked.

"Is the disability inclusion leader role still open?"

Kelly smiled. "I was hoping you'd ask me that. I held it open for you. You're the perfect person to lead it. Let's talk."

One Year Later

Kelly walked out on to the stage to applause of the packed auditorium. The audience quieted as Kelly began to speak.

"Colleagues, this was truly a banner year for us. We continue to be a market leader and workplace innovator. This year we want to recognize someone for her exemplary results in helping us to be a disability inclusive organization. Jade, come on out here!"

As Jade wheeled out, the audience went wild with applause, whistles, and cheers. In leading the disability inclusion initiative, she had gotten to know a lot of people around the company whom she wouldn't have met otherwise. She was respected for her passion, ability to get things done, and empathic leadership style.

Kelly went on, "When I first talked with Jade about leading the disability inclusion initiative she was, let's say, a bit apprehensive, right Jade?" Kelly smiled at Jade.

"Apprehensive--right," Jade said as she laughed.

"That evening, Jade was in a horrible accident. For nine months she had to re-learn and adjust nearly every aspect of her life. But Jade decided she didn't want to just get by, she wanted to thrive. When she came back to work, she accepted my offer to take on the disability inclusion initiative. I'm so proud to say that as a result of her leadership we are viewed as a disability inclusion thought leader. Our employee retention is up 15 percent, our number of employees with a disclosed disability is up 20 percent, our employee satisfaction is up 10 percent, and 100 percent of our managers have gone through training on how to create a disability inclusive workplace. And we're just getting started. Jade, do you have anything you want to say?"

"Actually, I do, Kelly. First, I want to thank the team of influencers: Annabelle Dang, Karen Hung, Todd Krell, Jim Peterson, Keith Wright, Dana Karila, and Jana Gomez who work with me each day to help all of you be more disability inclusive. Next, I want to thank our project manager Tyler Bell, for keeping us all on track. I also want to thank Kelly for providing outstanding leadership and support and doing whatever I asked her to do."

"It was my pleasure to work for you, Jade," Kelly said to some laughs from the audience.

Jade struck a serious tone. "You know, I've had a lot of ups and downs since the accident. I went through a period of pretty serious depression, starting from when I had to move back into my parents' place because of the stairs at my old apartment. There were days that I just didn't want to get out of bed. The worst was the day I gave away my bike. I hated seeing it go, but I was able to give it to a young woman who couldn't afford one of her own. I cried for days over it, but at the same time it was kind of a watershed moment for me. I knew that I had to accept my new normal, which is when I went out and bought a handcycle. I've been riding it every day and my goal is to do a 100-mile ride next summer."

"That's great, Jade," Kelly said as she wiped a tear.

Jade continued. "I also want to thank all of you for being so willing to change our DI DNA. Lastly, there are seven people I met on my journey who guided, encouraged, and inspired me to passionately take on the role. None of them are here in the auditorium, but they're in my heart forever. Thank you all!"

"Thank you, Jade! Colleagues, give Jade another round of applause!" Kelly said.

Jade wheeled off the stage, waving to the audience on the way. Kelly watched as Jade left, smiling at the gold door painted on the back of her wheelchair.

For more on how to create a disability inclusive organization go to DIchampion.com.

See a sample from *Behind Gold Doors-Five Legends Offer the Keys to Empowering Leadership*

Embossed Card

Sam had been dreading this meeting for days. He stood outside Karen's office waiting for her to finish her phone conversation. He could see her through the window in her door. She held up her index finger. Only one more minute before the dressing-down.

Karen hung up the phone and motioned Sam in.

"How's it going?" Sam said.

"Fine, thanks."

Karen got up from her desk and sat at a small round table with two chairs. Sam sat across from her and put his notebook and water bottle on the table.

"Sam, have you had a chance to review your performance appraisal?"

Sam opened his notebook. In it was a folded copy of the appraisal.

"I have."

"Good. Let's talk through strengths and areas for improvement."

Sam had always been an over-achiever. Graduating from college at age 20, he took great pride in how much he achieved at such a young age. He had been considered a rising star at the company since joining five years earlier. He was recently promoted to a management position, with an organization of ten people reporting to him. This was his first performance appraisal as a manager.

"So, let's first go through strengths," Karen said. Sam barely looked at the strengths, it was that one area for improvement that dominated his thoughts.

Karen continued. "Great delivery results, you come in on budget, customer satisfaction exceeds expectations. Great work." Karen continued with more specifics and comments from customers. Sam sat quietly as she talked, giving an occasional nod and *mm-hmm* to signal understanding.

"Enough with this, get on with the meat," he thought.

"Great, now let's talk about areas for improvement."

Sam leaned back in his chair, his hands gripping the armrests.

"Your organization's employee satisfaction surveys raised something we need to work on together."

Sam looked back at his manager score on the appraisal where his score was compared to other managers in the company. His score was among the lowest, with 95 percent of the managers scoring higher than him. It was the first time in his career he wasn't at the top of the heap, let alone being in the lowest five percent.

"In looking at the questions and comments, people seem concerned about your ability to empower others."

This was a total shock to Sam. He thought he did a great job of delegating and getting things done with his team. It wasn't just one person who said he didn't delegate effectively; it was a consensus among his team.

"I just don't understand this," Sam stammered. "I work so hard to make sure I am delegating work effectively." Karen and Sam continued to talk through the employee survey. To Karen, this was something for Sam to work on in his leadership journey. To Sam, it was like having bamboo stuck under his fingernails. Karen saw how this was impacting Sam; so she decided to make him an offer.

"Sam, you have great potential, and I want to ensure I'm doing my part to help you grow as a leader." Karen got up from the table, went back to her desk, opened the top drawer, took out a gold card, and sat back down at the table.

"There is a very special empowerment class I would like you to attend," Karen said as she handed him the card.

Sam looked at the card, a gold embossed door on the front, an address on the back. He recognized the address.

"This is a bakery; you want me to go to a class at a bakery?"

"Take tomorrow off. Go to the address on the card. They'll be waiting for you."

"Um, okay," Sam said. He had thought for sure he would be fired. Instead he was being sent to a class. Sam got up from the table, grateful he still had his job but perplexed by the gold card and what awaited him the next day.

"Thank you, Karen."

"Hang in there Sam, and let's get together after the class to talk about what you've learned."

"Okay." Sam left her office. As he walked to his office, he ran his thumb over the outline of the door on the embossed card. He flipped it over and looked at the address again.

"A bakery?"

See a sample from *Behind Gold Doors-Nine Crucial Elements to Achieve Good-Enough Contentment*

At This Time...

Ty got his morning coffee and turned on his computer. The first email was from one of the companies where he had sent his resume. He hovered the cursor over the email, took a deep breath, and double-tapped the track pad, opening the email.

Dear Mr. Taylor:
Thank you so much for your interest in Lake Industries. At this time…

Ty closed the email without reading further. They all started out with something like *"at this time," "unfortunately," or "we currently don't."* They ended with an empty *"we will keep your resume on file should something become available which matches your skillset. Thank you for your interest in blah-di-blah company."* He had gotten dozens of them, each one like a slug to the gut. Just as he shut his laptop Kate came into the kitchen. She immediately could tell what had happened.

"I'm so sorry, Ty," Kate said as she came around to him and put her hand on his shoulder. "Something will turn up; you just need to be patient."

Ty took a sip of coffee. "It's been six months and not one bite. Severance is gone, and the pittance we get from unemployment runs out next week. How much more patient do I need to be?"

"I wish I knew, honey. We're doing okay on finances and I've got plenty of client work in backlog. We've been through tougher times than this and we got through it. We'll get through this too." Kate poured herself a cup of coffee in a travel mug and took her lunch out of the fridge. "We'll talk more tonight, honey; I believe in you."

"I'm so lucky to have you," Ty said. "Do you want a lift to the train station?"

"I'll walk this morning, but how about you pick me up tonight? I should be on the 5:40, I'll call you if not."

"Got it, I love you."

Kate leaned over to kiss Ty. "Love you too."

Kate headed down the hallway to the front door. Ty heard the door open then gently click shut as she left.

His routine was the same every day. After Kate left for work, he'd finish going through his email inbox, then cruise the news websites, then up for a shower, then onto the job websites. As the weeks went by and the rejections piled up, he cast his job search net wider and wider; even looking at jobs that new college grads could do. He spent hours each day looking at opportunities, trying to network, and responding to job postings. Sometimes after lunch he would break routine and just sit on the couch with a bowl of chips watching afternoon talk shows. The couch sessions increased in frequency as he became more and more depressed. Most times he just wore sweats, since his pants had become too tight, but he knew better than to wear something with an elastic waistband if he and Kate were going out. He'd do the best he could to squeeze into his pants, preferring hooks over snaps to avoid them popping under pressure.

Socializing with friends was the worst. "How's the job search coming?" He'd hear it over and over. "Just great, pursuing a couple of opportunities," he'd lie, then try to change the topic. He particularly hated having to face his daughters and his shame of feeling like such a loser-unemployed dad.

Ty finished up his morning activities then made himself a tuna sandwich with chips and soda. "Wonder what's on TV this afternoon?" he said. "No, I need to work." He looked at his laptop, then the TV remote, then back at the laptop. "Actually, I need to get out." He finished his lunch, got his jacket and left the house for a walk.

"It's a beautiful Fall day," Ty said to himself as he walked down the street towards the train station. It was about a mile walk, one that he used to do every day when he worked at Conset, and the same that Kate did each day to get to her office. The street was lined with reddish-yellow trees that rained leaves onto the ground with each gust of wind. Ty took deep breaths as he walked, feeling the cool Autumn air fill his lungs. He walked by the park next to the train station. Two mothers with strollers sat on a bench talking. A man played fetch with his dog; on each throw the dog would run as fast as he could to the ball, kicking up a trail of leaves with each lunge. As he got closer to the train station, he noticed an old woman sitting in a wheelchair next to a bench. He slowed his walk to look at her. She wore a huge hat adorned with white flowers, a pink polka-dot sweater, and red and orange striped pants. On her lap sat a large paisley-print carpet bag. Her makeup looked as if it were applied with a putty knife. Her sunken eyes stared at Ty as he walked by, expressionless in her gaze, even though Ty smiled at her as he passed. As he continued to the station, he turned to look at the woman, who was still ogling him. Ty quickened his pace to get out of her eyeshot.

"Think I'll go into the city," Ty said to himself as he arrived at the train station. "I can make the 1:05, get into Chicago by 2, then Kate and I can ride the 5:40 back together.". He loved walking along Lakeshore Drive and experiencing the sights, smells and sounds of the expansive Lake Michigan. He bought a ticket and waited on the platform for the train to Union Station. The train's horn broke the silence of the Fall day as it approached the station; followed by the grinding of the metal wheels on the track as the train slowly approached the platform. He stood to board the train as it came to a stop. "How odd," he said to himself. The car was a familiar dingy silver, weathered by the countless trips around Chicagoland.

What wasn't so typical were the doors--gleaming gold, looking as if they were just delivered from the foundry and installed that day. The doors slid open, Ty boarded, then with a whoosh the doors closed behind him. He looked up and down the empty car and sat down in the seat next to the doors. Ty pulled out his phone, waiting for the train to depart. Just then the door abruptly opened.

"Help me!" Ty heard as he turned and looked back at the door.

See more at *behindgolddoors.com*

Acknowledgements

Behind Gold Doors: Seven Steps to Create a Disability Inclusive Organization was a labor of love not only from me but my many reviewers. Each of them guided the story, disability description accuracy, seven steps, and DIChampion.com content. Heartfelt thanks to Lindsay Perkins, Briana Sanger, Emily Ellis, Kimberly Drake, Christopher McMillan, Leo Ahearn, Amanda Thompson, Jae Kim, Jeanne Parish-Richardson, Mike Burkhalter, Jon Fleming, Louis Mendoza, Jim DuBois, Phil Peterson, Lori Lake, Stephanie Gebhardt, Emily Miller, Laura Kneedler, Steve Dunn, Mike Gano, Gene Boes, Rachel Nemhauser, and Gary Stobbe, MD. Special thanks to my editor and wife Patty Pacelli for the hours of reading, reviewing, cleaning up my bad English, and wise advice. Each contribution made the manuscript more interesting and credible. My deepest thanks to each of you.

Author note: The Lori character is the true-life story of my sister Lori Quaranta. The younger brother referred to in Lori's chapter is me. Lori survived her ruptured aneurysm but died of lung cancer 24 years later in 2012. Lindsay Perkins, one of the book reviewers, is Lori's daughter.

More Books on Leadership and Disability Inclusion

Want to be a leader others admire? Get the 12 simple leadership lessons the best leaders crush in *Why Don't They Follow Me?*

Need to be leader who truly empowers followers? See the four simple steps to intentional empowerment in *Behind Gold Doors-Five Legends Offer the Keys to Empowering Leadership*

Want your workplace to be more autism friendly? Get 100 lessons to create a welcoming workplace in *Six-Word Lessons for Autism Friendly Workplaces*

Want to relate better to your child with autism? See the 100 lessons to help dads in *Six-Word Lessons for Dads with Autistic Kids*

Want to see what it's really like growing up with autism? See how the author sees life in *Six-Word Lessons on Growing Up Autistic*

Want to help your child understand more about autism? Read *The Kindergarten Adventures of Amazing Grace* with your child

See Lonnie's Amazon Backlist at LPacelli.com

See more about Lonnie at LonniePacelli.com

References

[i] https://www.cdc.gov/ncbddd/disabilityandhealth/disability.html

[ii] https://www.who.int/mediacentre/news/notes/2012/child_disabilities_violence_20120712/en/

[iii] https://www.accenture.com/t20181029T185446Z__w__/us-en/_acnmedia/PDF-89/Accenture-Disability-Inclusion-Research-Report.pdf

[iv] http://www.businessanddisability.org/wp-content/uploads/2019/11/PDF_acc_FoW_PwD.pdf

[v] https://www.webmd.com/brain/brain-aneurysm#1

[vi] https://bafound.org/about-brain-aneurysms/brain-aneurysm-basics/brain-aneurysm-statistics-and-facts/

[vii] https://www.parkinson.org/Understanding-Parkinsons/Statistics

[viii] https://parkinsonsdisease.net/diagnosis/rating-scales-staging/

[ix] https://www.cdc.gov/ncbddd/cp/facts.html

[x] https://www.cerebralpalsyguidance.com/cerebral-palsy/research/facts-and-statistics/

[xi] https://www.rchsd.org/programs-services/cerebral-palsy-center/cerebral-palsy-facts-2/

[xii] https://www.afb.org/blindness-and-low-vision/eye-conditions/low-vision-and-legal-blindness-terms-and-descriptions

[xiii] https://www.nfb.org/resources/blindness-statistics

[xiv] https://www.webmd.com/brain/paralysis-types

[xv] https://www.christopherreeve.org/living-with-paralysis/stats-about-paralysis